Love to Sew

Quilted Covers & Cosies

Dedication

Dedicated to the loyal followers who buy my books. The
most satisfying part of my job is knowing that I have
given beginners a bit of help and encouragement, and
for the seasoned sewer, a little inspiration and a few
new ideas.

Love to Sew
Quilted Covers & Cosies

Debbie Shore

Search Press

First published in Great Britain 2016

Search Press Limited
Wellwood, North Farm Road,
Tunbridge Wells, Kent TN2 3DR

Text copyright © Debbie Shore 2016

Photographs © Garie Hind

Design copyright © Search Press Ltd. 2016

ISBN: 978-1-78221-254-6

The Publishers and author can accept no responsibility for any consequences arising from the information, advice or instructions given in this publication.

Suppliers
If you have difficulty in obtaining any of the materials and equipment mentioned in this book, then please visit the Search Press website for details of suppliers: www.searchpress.com

Templates
The templates for all the projects are provided at the end of the book and also on the Search Press website, www.searchpress.com

Acknowledgements

Thank you to my husband, Garie, for taking such amazing pictures, and Sophie from Search Press for putting this book together so beautifully!

Printed in China

Mug Hug, page 16

Egg Cosy, page 18

Umbrella Tea Cosy, page 26

Flower Tea Cosy, page 28

Phone Cover, page 34

Sunglasses Case, page 36

Tissue Box Cover, page 42

Toilet Paper Cover, page 46

Contents

Caravan Toaster Cover, page 20

Bird Coffee Cosy, page 24

Hot Water Bottle Cover, page 30

Tablet Sleeve, page 32

Book Cover, page 38

Bottle Cosy, page 40

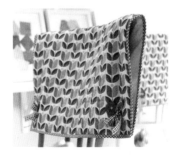

Contrast Coffee Cosy, page 50

Chair Back, page 54

Sewing Machine Cover, page 56

Straighteners Cover, page 58

Introduction

Fabric and textiles are the things that make me happy and thankfully keep me busy! Anything that involves sewing feeds my passion for stitching and still excites me even after half a century of sewing. My mum taught me to sew at a very young age, and I made dolls' clothes, then moved on to my own version of fashion – the 70s was such a fun era for glittery creations and spangly embellishments. After a long career in television, I now spend all my time happily designing patterns and projects that I love to share with you. The best part of my job is knowing that you have been inspired to start or restart sewing, and share my enthusiasm for anything stitched.

All of the projects in this book use a 0.5cm (¼in) seam allowance, unless stated otherwise. I like to use fusible fleece to give both stability and luxury to my fabrics. I have designed the projects as simply as I can so a beginner sewer will be able to make them, but if you are a seasoned sewer, you may like to add your own touch and personality to the items you make.

Covers and cosies are not just decorative projects; a tablet sleeve or phone cover can help to protect your screen, tea and coffee cosies will keep your drinks warm and a hot water bottle cover tends to be more snuggly than just the bottle itself. The main thing is to have a good time sewing, and enjoy the results.

Materials & equipment

Fabrics

I prefer to use 100% cotton quilting fabrics, available in such a wide range of prints and colours. Small prints are useful for small projects or appliqué, as you don't lose the pattern when you cut. Choose prints that complement each other and a few solid colours to break up the busyness of patterns.

Choose a good quality cotton and there will be less shrinkage. I don't usually pre-wash fabric that will end up being a project that can be spot cleaned, like my sewing machine dust cover, but if an item will be washed, for instance if used in the kitchen, it is always a good idea to pre-wash to avoid disappointment later.

Threads

Always use good quality thread – your project will last longer and the seams will be stronger. Good quality thread feels smother than poor quality, and will see less lint inside your sewing machine. Try to use cotton thread with cotton fabric, and the same thead in the top and bottom of your machine.

For hand sewing, use a stronger thread that can withstand pulling. Silk thread for appliqué gives a luxurious look and feel to your projects.

Sewing machine

There are many sewing machines on the market nowadays, with varied features and prices. If you are buying for the first time, I suggest a computerised machine. Although they usually cost more than a simple electronic machine, they are generally easier to use. Look for a needle up/down option, as this makes it easy to pivot around corners, and if you want to do free-motion embroidery, you will need a drop feed dog facility. For the projects in this book, you will need a straight stitch and an adjustable zigzag. You will also need a free-motion or darning foot. On the whole, the more stitches and features, the more costly the machine, so think carefully about where your sewing journey will take you, and shop wisely.

Wadding/batting

This is the layer that goes between the outer and lining fabrics. It is an important part of your quilting, even though you don't see it, as it adds a touch of luxury and drape to your fabric. It can help the covers and cosies to stand up firmly.

Choosing wadding/batting can be a bit of a minefield, but for the projects in this book, I have kept it quite simple. Terms you may see are ' loft' which is the thickness of the wadding, and 'scrim' which is the polyester layer that holds natural wadding together. Synthetics like polyester tend to have a higher loft, so the wadding is thicker. Nowadays you can even find synthetic wadding made from recycled plastic bottles! Natural wadding is made from cotton, wool, bamboo or soya, which tends to be softer and more breathable than synthetic.

Choose a fusible wadding that is ironed onto the back of your fabric to give it form and stability. If you can't find this, use a sew-in wadding and spray on repositionable fabric adhesive to hold it in place while sewing.

Also available on the market is a thermal wadding which I have used for tea and coffee cosies. For the hair straighteners cover, you need heat-reflective fabric as well as wadding. I used a piece of ironing board cover, which has the same effect.

I tend not to pre-wash wadding, but always follow the manufacturer's instructions.

The new kid on the block is foam stabiliser or fusible foam, which adds a real firmness to your project but is easy to sew through. It is perfect if you want the item to stand up alone and keep its shape.

Other materials

I try to keep materials to a minimum, as we're all on budget, but there are a few things that will make your sewing easier and your cutting accurate.

A good, sharp pair of **dressmaking shears** are worth the investment and can last you a lifetime if you look after them. **Pinking shears** are useful for snipping curves, and you will need small **embroidery scissors** for cutting threads.

You'll need **hand sewing needles**. I like to use sharps for most hand sewing and embroidery needles for thicker threads.

Cloth **tape measures** have a charm but may stretch with use, so go for a plastic one, in both centimetres and inches.

For accurate and quick cutting, a **rotary cutter, ruler and mat** are a godsend. The most useful size of rotary cutter is 45mm (1¾in), and go for as large a cutting mat and rectangular ruler as you have room for.

Repositionable spray fabric adhesive helps to keep appliqué flat when sewing. Make sure it is made for fabrics, as you don't want to damage your sewing machine.

A **seam ripper** is a must-have for those wonky stitched moments. They will blunt over time, so have a few in reserve in your sewing box.

You will also need **pins**, **piping cord**, **cotton webbing**, **buttons**, **ribbon**, **hair elastics**, **erasable pen**, **fusible adhesive**, **hook and loop fastening**, a **magnetic fasterner** and **paper, card** and **pen** for templates.

Basic techniques

Quilting

Quilting is the method of joining three layers together: outer fabric, wadding/batting and lining. The layers are stitched through by hand or machine to make a thick, padded, decorative material. Styles of quilting vary enormously, from traditional stippled quilts with a meandering stitch line that does not overlap itself, to abstract free-motion designs. You may choose any of the following styles for the projects in this book:

Outlining a patch or design

Following the lines of a motif on the fabric

Sewing straight lines

Sewing squares or diamonds to form a grid

See opposite how to measure angles for quilting grids.

Piecing, appliqué and decorative stitches can add interest to a quilted item, and there are no rules to say what type or colour of fabric you should use.

Measuring angles for quilting grids

To draw diagonal quilting lines onto your fabric, use a 45 degree angle. You will need a rectangular ruler with the correct markings.

Place the 45 degree mark across the bottom of your fabric and draw along the edge of the ruler (right) with erasable pen.
Use this line as a starting point for your grid.

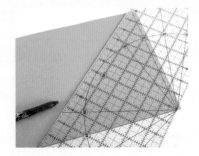

A 60 degree line (right) will give you a more elongated diamond. Always start in the centre of your fabric, to give a balanced look. Mark the centre point, and place your 60 degree mark on your ruler against the edge of the fabric. Draw a line along the edge of the ruler.

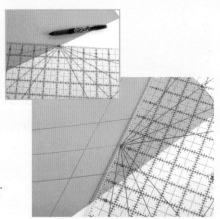

Piping

Piping adds the finishing touch to many projects and is very simple to make. You will need piping cord, which comes in many thicknesses, and a strip of bias-cut fabric. To gauge the width of fabric you need, multiply the width of the cord by two, then multiply the seam allowance by two and add the two together. So for the piping on my coffee cosy, I used 6mm (¼in) cord with a 6mm (¼in) seam allowance, I needed an 18mm (¾in) wide strip of fabric. If you are not sure, cut the strip a little wider; you can always trim it back.

Tip

If your piping is going round a curve or corner, snip into the seam allowance to allow the fabric to bend around the curve.

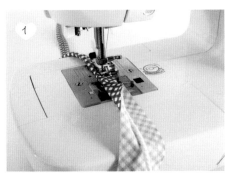

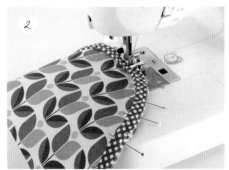

1 Wrap the fabric around the cord, and with the zipper foot on your machine, sew the raw edges together.

2 Place the edges of the trim to the edge of your fabric, and sew again, moving the needle closer to the cord.

3 Sew the second piece of fabric on top, right sides together, with the needle as close as you can to the cord but without sewing through it.

4 When you turn the item right side out, the piping should neatly finish the edge.

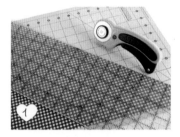
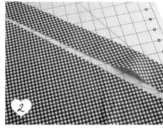
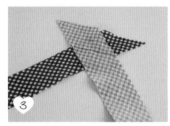

Bias binding

This is a simple solution to finish off raw edges, and gives a professional finish to your work. Although it can be bought in many colours and sizes, I like to make my own, as this is cost-effective and means I can coordinate my fabrics.

Bias binding is a strip of fabric cut on the diagonal, at a 45 degree angle, which allows a little 'give' so the fabric stretches around curves without puckering. To cut your fabric accurately, you need a rotary cutter, rectangular ruler and cutting mat.

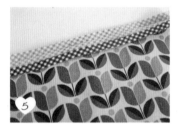

1 Lay your fabric squarely on the cutting mat, and place the 45 degree mark on your ruler on the straight edge of the fabric. Cut along it.

2 Turn your fabric over and use the straight side of the ruler to measure the width you need. For 2.5cm (1in) bias binding, you need to cut 5cm (2in) of fabric. As you are cutting the strips, the fabric will stretch, so fold it in half diagonally and cut through two, three or four layers at a time.

3 To join the strips, lay two pieces right sides together, overlapping at right angles. Draw a diagonal line from one corner to the other, as in the photograph. Pin, then sew along this line. Trim the raw edge back to around 3mm ($\frac{1}{8}$in) and press the seam open.

4 Bias binding involves folding over both of the long edges of the tape into the centre and pressing. The easiest way to do this is to use either a bias binding machine or a small bias tape maker. You thread the strip through this, it folds it in two and you press with your iron while pulling the fabric through. If you don't have a tape maker, carefully fold both long edges to the centre of the fabric strip and press. Be careful not to get your fingers too close to the iron!

5 To apply the binding, firstly open up the crease lines, and place on your project along the raw edge, right sides together. Pin, then sew with your machine along the first crease mark.

6 Now fold the tape over the raw edge, pin and use a slip stitch to sew the bias binding to the other side of the work by hand.

Joining ends

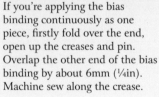

If you're applying the bias binding continuously as one piece, firstly fold over the end, open up the creases and pin. Overlap the other end of the bias binding by about 6mm (¼in). Machine sew along the crease.

Fold over and stitch as before, or instead of slip stitching by hand, you could machine top stitch.

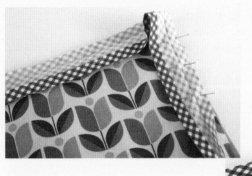

Mitring a corner

Bias binding will stretch around a curve, but if you want to mitre a corner, sew again along the crease line but stop 6mm (¼in) from the corner and back-tack to stop the stitches from coming undone. Fold the tape along the second side, making a triangular pleat in the corner.

Fold the pleat away from your stitch line, and sew straight down the second side. Open up the tape at the corner and you should see a neat mitre forming. As you fold the tape over, mirror the same mitre on the reverse.

Appliqué

Applique is the method of applying a decorative fabric motif to your work. This could be a hand-stitched felt shape, as with the embellishments on my toilet paper cover, patterns cut from pre-printed fabric like the flower tea cosy, or fabric shapes you have drawn freehand, or transferred from a template, as with my bird coffee cosy.

To make the application easier, use a repositionable spray fabric adhesive to keep the shapes in place, or iron a sheet of fusible adhesive to the back of the fabric before cutting. Then peel off the paper backing and re-iron the designs into position.

Felt appliqué looks charming when hand embroidered with a blanket or running stitch; the depth and texture of felt really makes the stitches stand out. Try hand stitching in blanket stitch around woven fabrics too – this gives a rustic look to your work.

For a neater look, use the blanket or pin stitch on your sewing machine.

If you are machine sewing, form a dense line by shortening your zigzag stitch to make it into a satin stitch. This will also help prevent woven fabrics from fraying.

Try your machine's blind hem stitch if you don't want to see so much of the stitch. Always test out the stitch you would like to use on scrap fabric first, to make sure you are happy with it.

Mug Hug

Materials

Measure your mug. Mine is 24cm (9½in) in circumference. Cut your fabric to this width. The height of my mug is 10cm (4in). Cut the fabric length 1cm (½in) less.

- ♥ piece of outer fabric, 24 x 9cm (9½ x 3½in)
- ♥ piece of lining the same size
- ♥ piece of wadding/batting the same size
- ♥ 69cm (27in) of 2.5cm (1in) bias binding
- ♥ 1 hair elastic
- ♥ 1 button
- ♥ 3 scraps of fabric for the birds
- ♥ repositionable spray fabric adhesive

Tools

- ♥ sewing machine, thread and free-motion foot
- ♥ fabric scissors
- ♥ iron
- ♥ erasable pen
- ♥ hand sewing needle

1 Fuse the wadding/batting to the back of the outer fabric.

2 Use the templates on page 63 to cut out bird shapes from the three scrap pieces of fabric. Spray with a little adhesive, and place at angles on the outer fabric. Draw the legs, wings, plumes beaks and eyes with erasable pen.

3 Put the free-motion foot on your sewing machine, drop the feed dogs and outline the details you drew in pen, with free-motion stitching. I find it looks better if I outline about three times.

4 Erase the ink outlines and press.

5 Sew the hair elastic in the centre of one short side, facing inwards.

6 Apply the bias binding all the way round the edges, mitreing the corners for a neat look (see pages 14–15).

7 Top stitch over the bungee so it is facing outwards.

8 Sew the button to the opposite side.

Egg Cosy

Materials

My egg cup measures 17.5cm (7in) around the widest part; alter the measurements or yours. For one egg cosy you need:

- 1 piece of blue fabric, 20 x 10cm (8 x 4in)
- 1 piece of pink fabric, 20 x 5cm (8 x 2in)
- 1 piece of lining fabric, 20 x 12.5cm (8 x 5in)
- 1 piece of wadding/batting, 20 x 12.5cm (8 x 5in)
- 2.5cm (1in) ribbon
- card and pen for template
- 2 small buttons
- pink embroidery thread

Tools

- sewing machine, thread and free motion foot
- iron
- fabric scissors
- erasable pen
- hand sewing needle

1 To make your template, draw a rectangle 10 x 11.5cm (4 x 4½in). Curve the top.

2 Sew the blue fabric to the pink and press. Back with wadding/batting. Cut in half. Place the template over the top and draw round the curved shape with the erasable pen.

3 Draw a flower shape in the centre of each piece. These don't have to be perfect, in fact they'd look great if the kids drew them!

4 Free-motion embroider over the design, in pink thread for the flower and green for the stalk and leaves, then add a button to the centre of the flower using the pink embroidery thread. Cut around the curved shape.

5 Use your template to cut out two lining pieces.

6 Sew the straight edge of the lining to the same of the outer pieces, right sides together. Fold the ribbon in half and sew, facing inwards, to the top of one outer piece.

7 Place the two sides of the cosy right sides together, matching lining to lining, and sew all the way round, leaving a gap in the lining for turning.

8 Turn the right side out, sew the opening closed, and push the lining inside the cosy.

9 Top stitch around the straight edge to neaten.

Caravan Toaster Cover

Materials

Measure the height, width and depth of your toaster and add 4cm (1½in) to each measurement. My toaster is 23cm (9in) long, 11.5cm (4½in) wide and 15cm (6in) high, so the cover is based on this size.

- 4 pieces of plain fabric (mine has a slight spot detail), 19 x 26.5cm (7½ x 10½in), to give 2 for the outside and 2 for the lining
- 2 pieces of wadding/batting the same size
- 2 pieces of plain fabric, 15 x 56cm (6 x 22in)
- 1 piece of wadding/batting the same size
- 2 pieces of striped fabric, 26.5 x 9cm (10½ x 3½in)
- 2 pieces of striped fabric, 15 x 9cm (6 x 3½in)
- 1 piece of coloured fabric for the door, 7.5 x 13cm (3 x 5in)
- 4 pieces of cream fabric for windows, 10 x 7.5cm (4 x 3in)
- 1 piece of cream fabric for the door window, 5cm (2in) square
- 1 piece of fabric, 2.5 x 5cm (1 x 2in) for the plant pot
- 8 pieces of fabric 5 x 7.5cm (2 x 3in) for the curtains
- 2 pieces of fabric (2in) square for the door curtains
- 8 small buttons to tie back the curtains
- 1 button for the door handle
- 3 flower-shaped buttons
- repositionable spray fabric adhesive

Tools

- sewing machine and thread
- iron
- fabric scissors
- rotary cutter, ruler and mat
- 5cm (2in) circle template
- erasable pen
- hand sewing needle

1 Fold over the top long edges of the four striped pieces of fabric by 0.5cm (½in) and press.

2 Place the corresponding sizes of striped fabric over the bottom of two of the plain 19 x 26.5cm (7½ x 10½in) rectangles and top stitch the pressed edges. Lay these pieces on top of the wadding/batting. One of these will be the front, and one the back of your caravan.

3 Draw horizontal lines with your erasable pen at 1cm (½in) increments from the top of the striped fabric to the top of the plain fabric, and sew. Using your circle template, round off the two top corners.

4 Take the long rectangle, place the corresponding piece of striped fabric over one end and top stitch the pressed edge. Add the same number of quilting lines as in step 3.

5 Spray the back of one window piece, and place it on the end of the long rectangle, overlapping the striped fabric slightly. Fold two pieces of curtain fabric in half and press. Place these, raw edges together, at the sides of the window. Fold back the edges as shown and satin stitch all the way round.

6 Sew a button onto each curtain as shown. Don't put the window on the opposite end just yet.

7 Repeat to add a window on the back of the caravan, slightly to one side.

8 Do the same with the window on the front of the caravan, placing it to one side of the fabric so there is room for the pot and door.

9 Add the door, and satin stitch all the way round. Using your 5cm (2in) circle template, round off the top of the door window.

10 Fold the two pieces of door curtain fabric in half and press, then place them over the door window and cut to the same shape. Satin stitch to secure. Add a button for the door handle.

11 Trim the bottom corners of the plant pot fabric to make a cone shape, and satin stitch to the side of the door. Draw stalks with your erasable pen, and stitch with a bold triple stitch on your machine, before adding your flower buttons.

12 Pin the front of the caravan to the window side of the long rectangle, lining up the striped section. Keep pinning all the way round, and trim any extra fabric when you come to the other end. This will make sure your centre panel is cut to the right length.

13 Unpin, then sew the striped panel, quilting lines, window and curtains on to the plain end of the strip.

14 Sew the front and back of the caravan, right sides together, to the long strip of fabric. This will form the box shape of your toaster cover.

15 With the remaining plain fabric, sew the two rectangles to the long strip of fabric, trimming off the excess at the end of the centre panel and leaving a gap in one side of about 10cm (4in) for turning.

16 Drop the outer fabric inside the lining, right sides together, and sew the raw edges together. Turn through the gap in the lining.

17 Push the lining inside the outer layer, press, then top stitch around the hem.

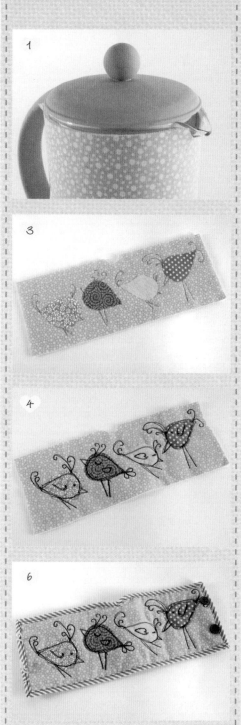

Bird Coffee Cosy

Materials

- 1 piece of outer fabric measuring the circumference of the pot – mine is 32cm (12½in), by the height of the glass section – mine is 11.5cm (4½in)
- 1 piece of lining the same size
- 1 piece of thermal fusible wadding/batting the same size
- 4 scraps of fabric, 7.5cm (3in) square
- 2 buttons
- 2 hair elastics
- 91cm (36in) bias binding
- repositionable spray fabric adhesive

Tools

- sewing machine, thread and free-motion foot
- fabric scissors
- erasable pen
- hand sewing needle
- iron

1 Fold your outer fabric in half and cut a small 'V' shape at the top of the fold to accommodate the coffee pot's spout. Check the fit.

2 Cut the same shape from the lining and wadding/batting. Fuse the wadding/batting to the back of the outer fabric.

3 Use the templates on page 63 to cut the scraps of fabric into bird shapes and arrange at angles across the outer fabric. Secure them with the spray. Draw on legs, plumes, beaks, eyes and wings with the erasable pen.

4 Free-motion embroider on your sewing machine a few times to outline and add detail to the birds.

5 Place this section wrong sides together with the lining, sew the two hair elastics facing inwards to one short end, spacing them equally, and apply the bias binding all the way round (see pages 14–15).

6 Fold back the hair elastics and top stitch so they face outwards. Sew the buttons to the opposite side to correspond.

Umbrella Tea Cosy

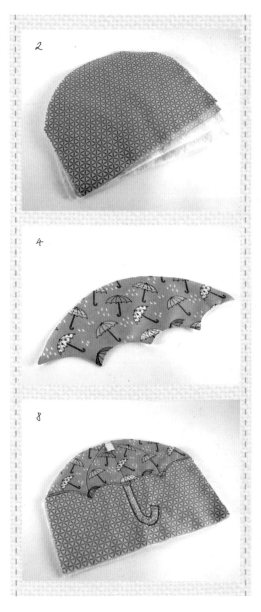

Materials

- ♥ 46cm (half a yard) of fabric for the cosy
- ♥ 46cm (half a yard) of umbrella print fabric for the umbrella and bias binding
- ♥ 46cm (half a yard) of fabric for the lining
- ♥ 15cm (6in) fabric scrap for the handle
- ♥ 23cm (a quarter yard) of thermal wadding/batting
- ♥ 5cm (2in) of ribbon

Tools

- ♥ sewing machine and thread
- ♥ fabric scissors and pinking shears
- ♥ large plate for template
- ♥ smaller circular template for the umbrella
- ♥ erasable pen
- ♥ iron

1 Measure the width and height of your teapot and add 5cm (2in) to each measurement. Cut two pieces each of cosy fabric and wadding (batting) to this size.

2 Draw and cut a curve at the top of the fabric and wadding/batting using the plate as a template. Fuse the wadding/batting to the back of the fabric.

3 Cut two pieces of umbrella fabric with the same curve, but this time 15cm (6in) deep. Fold in half then half again widthwise, mark the quarter lines with erasable pen, then use the smaller circle template to draw four curves on each piece.

4 Cut out the curves as shown to make the two umbrella shapes. Use these pieces as templates to cut the same shapes from lining fabric. Sew the umbrellas right sides together to the lining pieces, just around the small curves, leaving the top open.

5 Snip across the seam allowances at the points of the curves, turn the right side out and press.

6 Use the template on page 62 to cut out two 'J' shapes from the handle fabric, position in the centre of each side of the cosy, under the umbrella. Satin stitch all round.

7 Place the umbrellas over the handles, with the top edges meeting. Pin, then top stitch around the bottom of the umbrella. Draw lines from the centre top to the points of the umbrella, and top stitch. I used a triple straight stitch to make the lines stand out.

8 Fold the ribbon in half and sew, facing inwards, to the centre top of one cosy piece.

9 Sew the two cosy pieces right sides together, leaving the bottom edge open. Snip around the curves – pinking shears will come in handy! Turn the right side out and press.

10 Sew the two lining pieces right sides together in the same way and leave inside out.

11 Push the lining inside the outer layer. Pin the straight edges together, then cut 61cm (24in) of 2.5cm (1in) bias binding from the umbrella fabric and apply it round the raw edge (see pages 14–15).

Flower Tea Cosy

Materials

For a teapot measuring 25.5cm (10in) across:

- 2 pieces of outer fabric, 30.5 x 28cm (12 x 11in)
- 2 pieces of lining fabric the same size
- 2 pieces of thermal wadding/batting the same size
- 66cm (26in) of 2.5cm(1in) bias binding
- 25.5cm (10in) square of fabric for the semicircle appliqué
- patterned fabric scraps backed with fusible adhesive

Tools

- sewing machine, thread and free motion foot
- 24cm (9½in) circle template (I used a plate)
- iron
- 15cm (6in) circle template
- erasable pen

1 Using the smaller template, cut the two top corners of all fabrics and wadding/batting into curves.

2 Draw an arc on the front outer fabric with erasable pen, using the large circle template. Use the templates on page 62 to cut out appliqué shapes and arrange them around the arc, then iron in place. Draw stalks from the appliqué shapes, place the outer fabric on top of the wadding/batting, and free-motion embroider the shapes and stalks in a contrasting thread.

3 Fold the square fabric in half and draw an arc with the large circle template, with the fold just beyond the top of the arc. Cut the shape 6mm (¼in) larger than this. Sew the fabrics right sides together along the arc, leaving the straight edge open, then snip into the curve, turn the right side out and press.

4 Place this arc over the front fabric, and sew a few concentric arcs to quilt in place.

5 Place the remaining wadding/batting on the wrong side of the plain outer fabric piece and sew the two outer pieces right sides together, leaving the straight edge open. Snip into the curves, turn the right side out and press.

6 Sew the two lining pieces together around the curved sides. Push the lining, inside out, inside the tea cosy and tack/baste the raw edges together.

7 Apply the bias binding around the raw edge (see pages 14–15).

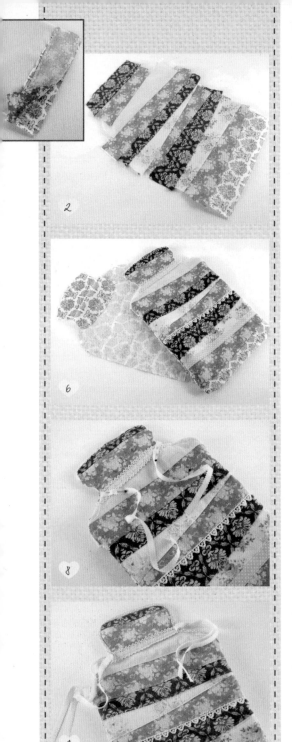

Hot Water Bottle Cover

Materials

For a 33 x 23cm (13 x 9in) bottle:
- 46 x 61cm (18 x 24in) wadding/batting
- 46 x 30.5cm (18 x 12in) calico
- fabric for the back, the same size
- 15 or so strips of fabric, lace and ribbon, various widths, at least 28cm (11in) long
- 46 x 61cm (18 x 24in) fabric for lining
- 81cm (32in) ribbon for ties
- 107cm (42in) bias binding

Tools
- sewing machine and thread
- card and pen for template
- scissors

1 Draw round the hot water bottle on the card, leaving a border of around 5cm (2in) all the way round. Cut out the template, then fold in half lengthways to make sure it is symmetrical. Use to cut one shape from the calico, one from the fabric for the back and two from the lining fabric.

2 Take the first strip of fabric and lay it right side up across the bottom of the calico. Place the second strip right side down, overlapping the first at a slight angle, and sew across the top. Flip the other strip right side up and press. Repeat until all the calico is covered.

3 Stitch strips of ribbon or lace across the seams. Don't use scratchy lace!

4 Place this piece of the hot water bottle cover right side up on top of one piece of wadding/batting. Lay the fabric for the back right side down on top, then finally the second piece of wadding/batting.

5 Sew together, from the curve of the 'shoulder', round the bottom and up to the same point on the other shoulder, leaving the top open to slip the hot water bottle inside. Quilt each side of the seams, using a decorative stitch if you like, then trim the excess fabric back to the shape of the calico.

6 Place the lining fabrics right sides together and sew in the same way.

7 Turn the outer bag the right way out. Push the lining, inside out, inside the main cover, which should now be right side out.

8 Cut the ribbon into four, then pin each piece facing inwards to the neck of the cover.

9 Pin then sew the bias binding around the opening, trapping the ribbon in the stitching (see pages 14–15. Take out the pins and put the filled hot water bottle inside.

Tablet Sleeve

Materials

These dimensions fit my tablet but of course measure yours.

- 1 piece of outer fabric, 21.5 x 27cm (8½ x 10½in) for the front panel
- 1 piece of lining the same size
- 1 piece of fusible wadding/batting the same size
- 1 piece of outer fabric, 21.5 x 34.5cm (8½ x 13½in) for the back panel
- 1 piece of fusible wadding/batting the same size
- 1 piece of lining fabric the same size
- 2.5cm (1in) of hook and loop fastening
- fabric scraps: stripes for the beach hut and roof, colours for bunting and door, yellow for the sand, blue for the sea, and orange for the sun
- button for the door handle

Tools

- sewing machine, thread and free-motion foot
- rotary cutter, ruler and mat
- iron
- 5cm (2in) circle template

1 Fuse the wadding/batting to the pieces of outer fabric.

2 Cut the striped beach hut fabric into a rectangle, about 10 x 13cm (4 x 5in), fold in half and cut to a point to shape the roof. Cut two orange circles for the sun, using your 5cm (2in) circle template. You will need five or six triangles for the bunting. I have used striped fabric for the beach hut roof and my door measures 5 x 7.5cm (2 x 3in).

3 Place a strip of blue fabric across the front panel outer fabric to make the sea, then slightly overlap with the yellow fabric for sand. Assemble all the appliqué pieces.

4 Sew in place, using free-motion stitches to make waves in the sea, a cloud in the sky and a string for the bunting. I have left the appliqué fabric raw at the edges to fray a little. Add the hook and loop fastening to the centre, 2.5cm (1in) from the top. Stitch on the button.

5 Take the outer piece for the back panel, and fold it over your decorated front fabric to gauge where the flap will sit. Place the second sun over the first, trim away the excess fabric and sew in place.

6 Sew the second part of the fastening to the centre of the back panel lining fabric, 2.5cm (1in) from the top.

7 Place the decorated front panel and its lining fabric right sides together and sew across the top. Turn over and press. Top stitch.

8 Lay the front and back panels right sides together and sew down one side.

9 Place this section on top of the final lining piece, with the fastening at the top and the decorated panel sandwiched in the middle. Sew all the way round, leaving a turnign gap of about 7.5cm (3in) in the side corresponding to the seam in step 8.

10 Turn the right side out and press. Top stitch all around, closing the turning gap.

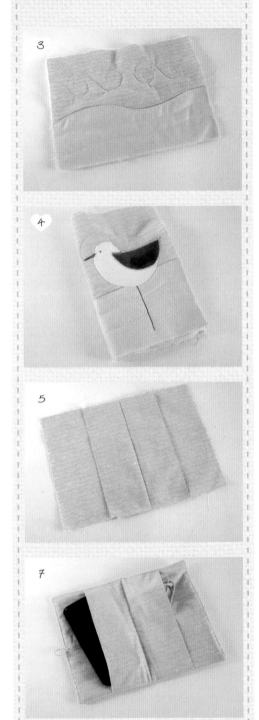

Phone Cover

Materials

- 3 pieces of blue outer fabric, the height of your phone plus 2.5cm (1in) by the width plus 2.5cm (1in) – mine are 23 x 18cm (9 x 7in)
- 2 pieces of yellow fabric, 23 x 9cm (9 x 3½in)
- 1 piece of fusible wadding/batting, 23 x 18cm (9 x 7in)
- 1 circle of white fabric, 7.5cm (3in) across
- A semicircle of grey fabric, 6cm (2½in) across
- 1 hair elastic
- 1 small button
- orange embroidery thread

Tools

- sewing machine and thread
- scissors
- rotary cutter, ruler and mat
- hand sewing needle
- iron

1 Fuse the wadding/batting to the back of one blue rectangle (for the front panel).

2 Put the yellow fabric right sides together. Draw a wave shape across the top. Stitch the wave, trim the excess fabric, turn right side out and press.

3 Top stitch this sand section across the front panel. Sew a few swirls with a machine straight stitch and white thread, for waves in the sea and wavy lines across the sand.

4 Cut an 'S' shape in the top of the white fabric to make it a bird shape, place on the right-hand half of your front panel and satin stitch in place. Put the grey semicircle as a wing over the top and satin stitch. Use a triple straight stitch on the machine with orange-brown thread to draw a leg and beak. Hand stitch a French knot for the eye.

5 Take one of the remaining blue fabrics and sew the short edges together to make a tube. Turn through and press, with the seam at the back. Place centrally on top of the final piece of blue fabric, and sew down the middle.

6 Sew through the centre of one side to make two smaller pockets. Place the front and back sections right sides together and add the hair elastic facing inwards in the centre of one side. Sew all the way round, leaving a gap of about 7.5cm (3in) for turning.

7 Turn the right side out and press. Top stitch down the spine and all around the edge; this will close the opening.

8 Add a button to the opposite side to the hair elastic.

Sunglasses Case

Materials

- 20.5cm (8in) square of outer fabric
- 20.5cm (8in) square of lining fabric
- 20.5cm (8in) square of wadding/batting
- 86cm (34in) of 2.5cm (1in) bias binding
- 2 buttons, one smaller than the other

Tools

- sewing machine, thread and free-motion foot
- scissors
- hand sewing needle

1 Place the outer fabric over the wadding/batting, put the free-motion foot on your sewing machine and embroider around the print. I like to go over the same line two or three times.

2 Draw round a plate to help ou cut a curve across the top right corner, and do the same with the lining fabric square.

3 Mark the bottom centre point and start to sew the bias binding around the edge from this point, finishing halfway down the curved side (see pages 14–15). Make sure you leave a little extra binding at the ends to turn in.

4 Fold the case in half, take the bias binding over the edge, and hand-sew to finish. Wrap the tape over all layers of fabric from under the curve and across the base to make the case.

5 Add the buttons over the join, to decorate.

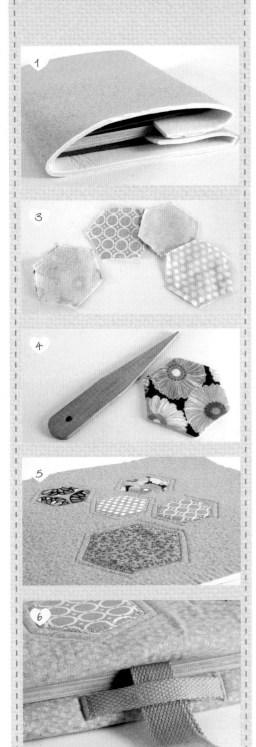

Book Cover

Materials

Measure your book. Mine is 28cm (11in) tall and 20.5cm (8in) wide. Cut your fabric the height of the book plus 5cm (2in) by twice the width plus 18cm (7in).

- 1 piece of outer fabric, 59 x 33cm (15 x 13in)
- 1 piece of lining fabric the same size
- 1 piece of foam stabiliser the same size
- 114cm (45in) of 2.5cm (1in) bias binding
- 46cm (18in) cotton webbing
- 4 pieces of contrasting fabric, 10cm (4in) square, for the small hexagon appliqué
- 1 piece of contrasting fabric, 15cm (6in) square for the large hexagon
- calico or scrap fabric to back the hexagons
- repositionable spray fabric adhesive

Tools

- sewing machine and thread
- rotary cutter and mat
- bamboo creaser
- scissors
- erasable pen

1 Spray the back of the outer fabric with adhesive, and place over the foam, smoothing out any wrinkles. Wrap this around your book, tucking the ends inside the book cover as shown.

2 Mark the area around the front of the cover with erasable pen, to give an outline in which to add the appliqué. Take the book out of the cover.

3 Use the templates on page 64 to cut out four small hexagon shapes, and one large, from both the contrasting fabric and calico. Sew the fabric and calico pieces right sides together. Snip a hole into the calico side of each one.

4 Turn through the hole, push out the corners with your bamboo creaser and press.

5 Arrange these on the front of your cover, securing in place with spray adhesive. Using a blanket stitch on your sewing machine, sew around each hexagon. With a straight stitch, add an outline 6mm (¼in) outside each hexagon.

6 Wrap the cover around your book again, and mark the centre of the open ends where the handle will attach. Cut a 7.5cm (3in) strip of cotton webbing, fold in half lengthwise and sew together along one long edge. Some webbing frays easily; if yours does, burn the ends carefully over a candle to seal them. Loop the remaining webbing, and with a satin stitch, attach to the centre front of the cover. Sew the shorter piece to the opposite side, parallel to the edge, for the loop to thread through.

7 Take the book out of the cover. Place the lining and outer cover wrong sides together. Sew bias binding along both short sides (see pages 14–15).

8 Fold the sides of the cover inwards by 7.5cm (3in), check the fit, then tack/baste. These pockets will hold the book cover. Apply the bias binding along the two long sides.

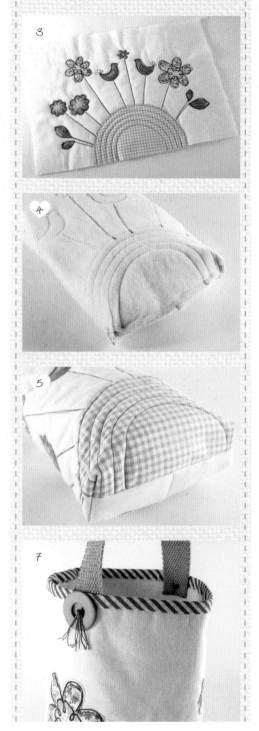

Bottle Cosy

Materials

- outer fabric, 33 x 38cm (13 x 15in)
- lining fabric measuring the same
- wadding/batting measuring the same
- scraps of patterned fabric backed with fusible adhesive for the appliqué
- 23cm (9in) square of fabric for the arc appliqué
- 30.5cm (12in) cotton webbing for the handle
- 2 large buttons
- 41cm (16in) of 2.5cm (1in) bias binding
- embroidery thread

Tools

- sewing machine, thread and free-motion foot
- fabric scissors and pinking shears
- 20cm (8in) circle template (I used a side plate)
- erasable pen
- hand sewing needle
- iron

1 As for the Flower Tea Cosy (page 28), draw an arc in the bottom centre of the outer fabric using the circle template. Use the templates on page 62 to cut the bird, flower and leaf shapes from the adhesive-backed patterned fabric, then arrange these around the arc. Iron them in place and draw stalks joining them to the arc. Place the wadding/batting underneath and free-motion embroider around the shapes and along the stalks.

2 Cut out two semicircles from the square fabric, 6mm (¼in) larger than the template. Sew the curved sides together, snip into the curve, turn the right side out and press.

3 Place into position on the decorated fabric panel and top stitch in place, adding a few concentric circles to create texture.

4 Fold the piece in half, right sides together and sew into a tube. With the seam in the centre, sew across the bottom. Pinch the ends of the bottom seam and sew across, 2.5cm (1in) from the point. This will square off the base of the cover.

5 Turn the right side out.

6 Make up the lining in the same way, but leave it inside out. Drop this inside the outer piece, and tack/baste around the top before adding the bias binding (see pages 14–15).

7 Pin the webbing either side of the inside of the cover, and attach by sewing straight through the buttons on the outside with the embroidery thread.

Tissue Box Cover

Materials

- 2 pieces of outer fabric, 25.5 x 10cm (10 x 4in)
- 2 pieces of foam stabiliser the same size
- 2 pieces of lining fabric the same size
- 2 pieces of outer fabric 14 x 10cm (5½ x 4in)
- 2 pieces of lining fabric the same size
- 2 pieces of foam stabiliser the same size
- 1 piece of outer fabric, 25.5 x 14cm (10 x 5½in)
- 1 piece of lining fabric the same size
- 1 piece of foam stabiliser the same size
- 81cm (32in) of 2.5cm (1in) bias binding
- 7.5cm (3in) square of felt for the heart
- embroidery thread
- repositionable spray fabric adhesive

Tools

- sewing machine and thread
- fabric scissors
- erasable pen
- embroidery needle for hand sewing
- ruler
- iron

1 Measure the centre point of the 25.5 x 14cm (10 x 5½in) piece of foam stabiliser and mark with your erasable pen. Place the oval template (see page 64) centrally over this mark and draw round it.

2 Take the lining and outer fabrics of the same size. Lay the lining right side up, place the outer fabric right side down on top, then the foam on top of this.

3 Sew round the marked oval shape, through all three layers. Cut out the hole in the centre, quite close to the stitches.

4 Push the lining through the hole. Press carefully with the iron while pulling the lining so that it sits flat.

5 Blanket stitch around the hole with embroidery thread. You can sew it on your machine first if you like, to hold the layers of fabric in place.

6 Take the four remaining outer pieces, and adhere them to their coordinating foam pieces with spray adhesive.

7 Draw a wavy line across all four pieces with your erasable pen, lining up the wave on each piece so that when the box is constructed, it goes continuously around the box. Embroider a running stitch along these lines, through the fabric and foam.

8 Use the template on page 64 to cut out the heart shape from felt, and place on one long side. Blanket stitch to secure.

9 Take all four side pieces and sew them to the top, avoiding sewing the lining for the top section into the seams.

10 Sew the side panels together to form the box shape.

11 Now sew the four lining pieces to the top lining piece, then sew the sides together. You should have two boxes joined together with the stitching around the oval-shaped hole.

12 Turn the outer box over the lining. Apply the bias binding around the bottom (see pages 14–15).

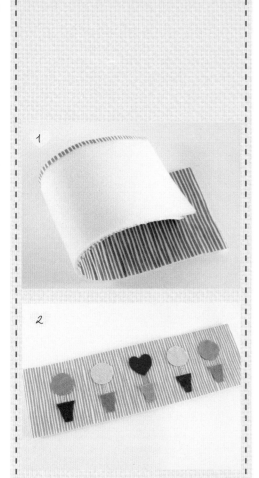

Toilet Paper Cover

Materials

My toilet roll measures 38cm (15in) in circumference, and is 10cm (4in) tall

- 1 piece of outer fabric, 44.5 x 14cm (17½ x 5½in)
- 1 piece of lining fabric, 44.5 x 15cm (17½ x 6in)
- 1 piece of fusible foam stabiliser, 44.5 x 13.5cm (17½ x 5¼in)
- circle of outer fabric, 15cm (6in) across
- circle of fusible foam stabiliser, 13.5cm (5¼in) across
- circle of lining fabric, 13.5cm (5¼in) across
- small pieces of green, brown, red and grey felt
- red and green embroidery thread
- 45.5cm (18in) of ribbon in three colours
- spray fabric adhesive

Tools

- sewing machine and thread
- fabric scissors
- embroidery needle for hand sewing
- iron

1 Fuse the rectangular foam to the outer fabric, aligning the sides and lower edge. Turn over the top of the fabric and glue in place.

2 Use the templates on page 64 to cut circles of green felt, a red felt heart, and brown felt pots. Add a small piece of ribbon for the tree trunks.

3 Hand-sew the felt shapes to the outer fabric with blanket or running stitch. I have added a few daisy stitch leaves too. A row of tiny stitches meandering between the pots adds extra texture.

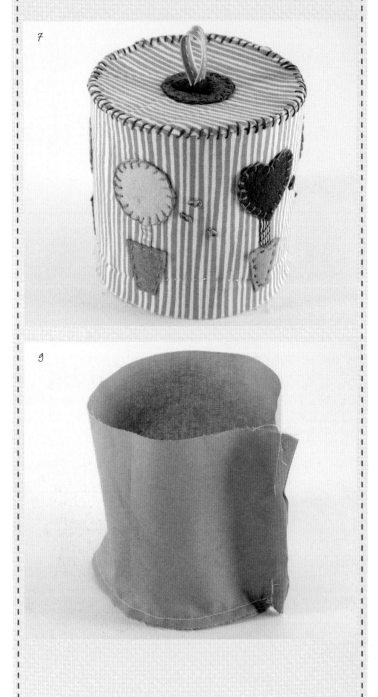

7

9

4 Sew the two short ends right sides together to make a tube. Turn the right side out.

5 Fuse the outer fabric circle to the foam, overlap the edge and glue.

6 Cut a green felt circle, then a small red heart. Place the heart on top of the circle, cut a hole in the centre, going through both, and loop a piece of ribbon through the hole to make a handle. Glue the ribbon in place at the back, and when dry, sew the handle centrally to the top of the holder.

7 Place the circle on top of the tube, and stitch them together by hand using contrasting embroidery thread.

8 For the lining, sew the short ends of the long piece together to make a tube, leaving a gap of about 7.5cm (3in) for turning.

9 Sew the circle to one end.

10 Drop the outer holder inside the lining, right sides together, and sew all the way round the raw edges.

11 Turn the right side out through the gap, then hand sew the gap closed.

12 Push the lining inside the holder. As the lining is longer, it will leave a 6mm (¼in) border around the bottom. Top stitch to neaten.

Contrast Coffee Cosy

Materials

Measure the height and width of your coffee pot, then add 5cm (2in) to each. Mine is 23cm (9in) tall including the lid, and 19cm (7½in) from spout to handle.

- 2 pieces of outer fabric, 28 x 24cm (11 x 9½in)
- 2 pieces of lining fabric the same size
- 2 pieces of thermal wadding/batting the same size
- 2 strips of contrast fabric 1, 30.5 x 12.5cm (12 x 5in)
- 2 strips of contrast fabric 2, 12.5 x 25cm (5 x 10in)
- 2 strips of contrast fabric 3, 7.5 x 12.5cm (3 x 5in)
- 61cm (24in) of 2.5cm (1in) bias binding
- 71cm (28in) of 6mm (¼in) piping cord
- 71cm (28in) of 4cm (1½in) bias binding
- 2 buttons to decorate, one larger than the other

Tools

- sewing machine and thread
- iron
- 30.5cm (12in) plate to use as a template
- hand sewing needle and thick thread
- erasable pen

1 For each side of the cosy, place the outer fabric on top of the wadding/batting and sew parallel straight lines across to quilt – as many as you like, no particular width apart. Lay contrast fabric 1 right side down at an angle, about 12.5cm (5in) from the bottom left corner as shown, and sew along the lower long edge.

2 Flip the contrast fabric over, and press. Sew straight lines through all the layers again, no particular width apart.

3 Place contrast fabric 2 right side down in the opposite direction, and sew as before.

6

7

8

4 Flip over contrast fabric 2, and quilt as before. Add contrast fabric 3 to the bottom left corner in the same way.

5 Trim away the excess fabric. Using your plate as a template, draw then cut the rounded shape of the top of the cosy.

6 Wrap the wide bias binding round the piping cord (see Piping on page 13). Snip into the seam allowance of the bias binding to allow it to curve, and sew it edge to edge with one side of your cosy, leaving out the straight bottom edge. Trim any excess length of piping.

7 Place the second side of the cosy on top, right sides together, and sew around the curved side, close to the piping. Turn the cosy right side out and press. Add the buttons at this point.

8 Sew the two lining pieces right sides together, leaving the straight bottom edge open.

9 Push the lining inside the cosy, wrong sides together, and sew together, very close to the edge. This helps to keep the fabrics in place while you add the bias binding at the bottom. Sew the 2.5cm (1in) bias binding around the bottom of the cosy (see pages 14–15).

Chair Back

Materials

Measure the widest part of your chair back – mine is 43cm (17in) – and add 10cm (4in). The cover can be as long as you like; mine is 33cm (13in) when finished.

- 1 piece of outer fabric, 53 x 66cm (21 x 26in)
- 1 piece of wadding/batting the same size
- 1 piece of lining fabric the same size
- 2.2m (86in) of 2.5cm (1in) bias binding
- 61cm (24in) ribbon for the bows
- 2 large buttons
- 2 x 2.5cm (1in) strips of hook and loop fastening

Tools

- sewing machine and thread
- rotary cutter, ruler and mat
- erasable pen

1 If your fabric has a directional print, cut it in half and join the two sides so that they are mirror imaging each other. This way, when the cover is folded over the chair back, the pattern will be the right way up on both sides. This also means you will have to trim the length of the lining and wadding/batting to fit.

2 With your erasable pen, draw vertical lines 5cm (2in) apart across the fabric. I fitted the lines into the pattern of my fabric.

3 Place the wadding/batting on the back of the fabric, and sew along the lines.

4 Place this layer wrong sides together with the lining and pin then tack/baste close to the edge.

5 Apply the bias binding all the way round (see pages 14–15).

6 Fold the cover over your chair back, pinch the front and back together and mark where the hook and loop fastening should go. Mine is 7.5cm (3in) from the bottom corners.

7 Sew the hook and loop fastenings to the lining side.

8 On the outer side, sew the buttons over the hook and loop stitches, then add a bow just below. You can choose whether this is the front or the back of your cover, or add buttons and bows to both sides if you wish!

Sewing Machine Cover

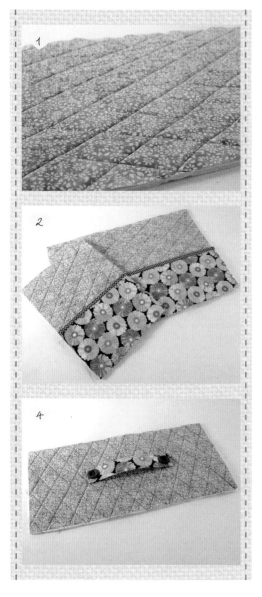

Materials

Measure the height, depth and width (at its widest part) of your sewing machine and add 4cm (1½in) to each measurement. Mine is 43cm (17in) wide, 29cm (11½in) high and 18cm (7in) wide.

- 2 pieces of outer fabric, 47 x 33cm (18½ x 13in)
- 2 pieces of foam stabiliser the same size
2 lining pieces, 46.5 x 33cm (18¼ x 13in)
- 2 pieces of outer fabric, 21.5 x 33cm (8½ x 13in)
- 2 pieces of foam stabiliser, 21.5 x 33cm (8½ x 13in)
- 2 pieces of lining, 21 x 33cm (8¼ x 13in)
- piece of outer fabric, 47 x 21.5cm (18½ x 8½in)
- piece of foam stabiliser, 47 x 21.5cm (18½ x 8½in)
- piece of lining fabric, 46.5 x 21cm (18¼ x 8¼in)
- piece of foam stabiliser, 20.5 x 5cm (8 x 2in) for the handle
- piece of fabric, 25.5 x 10cm (10 x 4in) for the handle
- 2 buttons
- 4 pieces of fabric, 47 x 15cm (18½ x 6in) for the side pockets
- 4 pieces of fabric, 21.5 x 15cm (8½ x 6in) for the side pockets
- 3m (3¼yd) of 2.5cm (1in) bias binding

Tools

- sewing machine and thread
- iron
- rectangular ruler
- erasable pen

1 Take each outer fabric piece, and starting in the centre, draw diagonal 60 degree lines, 4cm (1½in) apart (see page 13). Draw lines in the opposite direction to make a grid of diamonds. Place each piece of outer fabric over its coordinating foam piece, and top stitch along the lines.

2 With the wrong sides together, sew the pocket pieces together in pairs, and add the bias binding to the top (see pages 14–15). Tack/baste to the quilted outer pieces, and top stitch dividers to make pockets any size you like.

3 Sew all four outer pieces together to make a tube. Turn the right side out, and top stitch over the seams, close to the edge, to help them stay in shape.

4 Wrap the handle fabric around the foam, tucking in the raw edge, and sew all the way round. Sew this centrally to the top of the cover, lifting it slightly to make an arc shape, then add a button to each end.

5 With the cover inside out again, pin then sew in the top. Turn the right side out.

6 Make up the lining in the same way, then drop inside the cover, wrong sides together, and tack/baste around the edge. Add bias binding to finish.

Straighteners Cover

Materials

- 1 piece of outer fabric, 35.5 x 38cm (14 x 15in)
- 1 piece of fusible wadding/batting the same size
- 1 piece of heat-reflective fabric for the lining, the same size
- 1 piece of fabric for the pocket, 38 x 10cm (15 x 4in)
- I piece of wadding/batting the same size
- 1 piece of heat-reflective fabric the same size for the pocket lining
- 2 pieces of ribbon measuring 25.5cm (10in) each
- 1 magnetic fastener
- 1 x 5cm (2in) square of contrasting fabric

Tools

- sewing machine and thread
- rotary cutter, ruler and mat
- scissors
- fabric glue
- circular template measuring 7.5cm (3in) across; I used a ribbon reel
- erasable pen

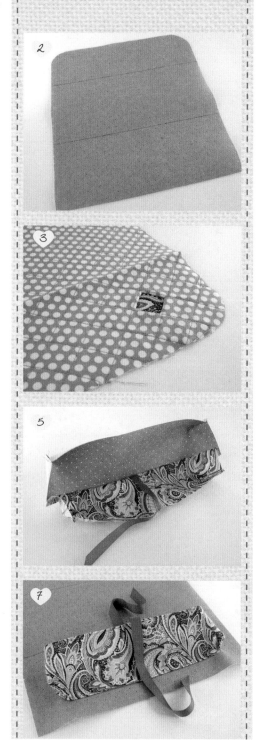

1 Fuse the wadding/batting to the wrong sides of your outer fabric and pockets. Using your circle template and pen, cut an arc from the top corners of your fabric (on one of the shorter sides). Repeat with the lining.

2 Measure 13cm (5in) from the bottom of the heat-reflective lining and draw a line in erasable ink, then another 14cm (5½in) above that. These are your fold lines. Attach the smaller half of the magnetic clasp centrally to the curved side of the lining, 2.5cm (1in) from the edge.

3 Draw diagonal lines at 45 degrees to the edges, 2.5cm (1in) apart (see page 13), over the front of the fabric to make a grid, then quilt over these lines. Cut a cross shape inside one of the squares, from the front of the cover. Fold back the points and glue them in place. Place the small piece of contrast fabric behind the hole, and again, glue. You could do this with several of the quilted squares if you wish.

4 For the pocket, cut a 2.5cm (1in) square from the bottom corners of both the outer fabric and lining. Pinch the sides of these squares together to form darts.

5 Pin one piece of ribbon, facing inwards, centrally to the top of the fabric. Sew the two pieces together across the top, trapping the ribbon in between.

6 Sew the pocket and lining together all the way round, leaving a gap of about 7.5cm (3in) in the bottom for turning. Make sure you don't catch the free end of the ribbon in the stitching. Clip across the corners, then turn the right side out and press. Top stitch across the straight top edge.

7 Pin the pocket centrally, 2.5cm (1in) from the bottom of the reflective lining, pulling the side in slightly to create a box shape. Sew in place. Sew the second piece of ribbon to the lining, just underneath the pocket, in line with the ribbon on the pocket.

8 Place the lining and outer fabric wrong sides together, fold along the fold lines, and mark where the second half of the magnetic clasp will fit, on the outer fabric. I find it easier to measure and mark this way so that I know it will be in the right place. Attach the clasp.

9 Place the two parts right sides together and sew all the way round, leaving a gap in one side for turning. Turn the right side out and press, then top stitch all the way round.

The closed Straighteners Cover, and (below) the open cover.

Templates

The templates for the Flower Tea Cosy (page 40) and the Bottle Cover (page 28)

The template for the umbrella handle for the Umbrella Tea Cosy (page 26)

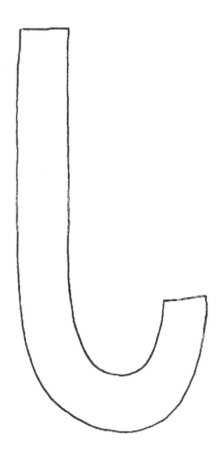

The bird templates for the Bird Coffee Cosy (page 24) and the Mug Hug (page 16)

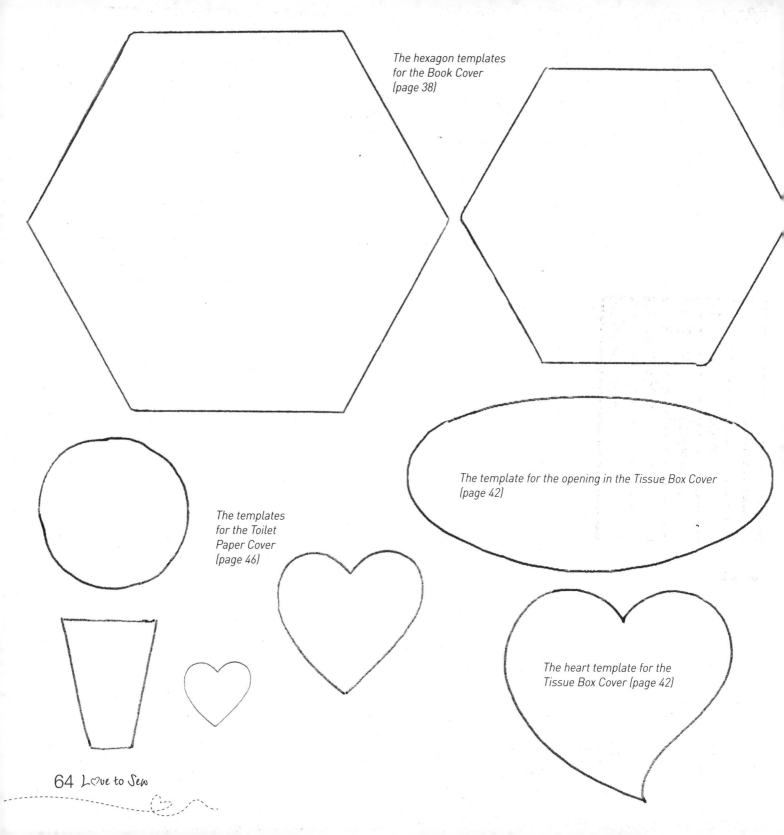

*The hexagon templates
for the Book Cover
(page 38)*

*The template for the opening in the Tissue Box Cover
(page 42)*

*The templates
for the Toilet
Paper Cover
(page 46)*

*The heart template for the
Tissue Box Cover (page 42)*